MW01713373

HARRY T. COOK

Sermons of a Devoted Heretic

A priest offers messages of hope to faithful doubters

CLAWSON, MICHIGAN

For more information, contact: The Center For Rational Christianity, PO Box 182, Clawson, Michigan 48017; phone (248) 588-1142.

To order additional copies of this book, contact:

The Cathedral Book Shop
4800 Woodward Avenue
Detroit, Michigan 48201
(313) 833-7545

Library of Congress Catalog Card Number: 99-93223

Cook, Harry T.
Sermons of a Devoted Heretic / Harry T. Cook — 1st Ed.

ISBN 0-9660728-1-2

Editor/Designer: Susan M. Chevalier
Proofreader: Emily Everett

Table of contents

PART TWO: SERMONS FOR SPECIAL OCCASIONS

BAPTISM

COMMUNION

ADVENT

Preface

"For everything there is a season," wrote the sage who gave us Ecclesiastes. Among other temporal enterprises, he insisted, is "a time to seek." For those who would embrace or even edge close to Christianity at the end of the 20th century, it is surely a time to seek, to question, to confess doubt and to admit of the necessity of the rational approach. Matters of religion are too important to abandon to the whims of emotion or what some call "spirituality," in which, it seems, whatever one feels bubbling up from within is valid and is to be taken seriously by others, because "everyone is entitled to his or her own opinion" or to experience a feeling and pronounce it a shaft of divine revelation.

The sermons in this book were preached to a congregation whose members are struggling — struggling with a priest who is himself struggling with the necessity (as he perceives it) of recasting traditional beliefs in language and concept that make sense on the verge of a new millennium. By no means were these sermons uniformly well-received. Indeed, one or two of them became the presenting reason for some people to leave the fellowship of the congregation. I am told that one or two former members are considering charging me formally with heresy. "Heresy" is a Greek word that means "choice." Thus a heretic is one who has chosen. In that sense, I am already guilty as charged — though a public trial would do wonders for book sales.

Conversely, these same sermons have been deliverance for what I call "faithful doubters," not quite religion's "cultured despisers" but ones who hang on tenuously to organized religion and at least the form, if not the substance, of its traditions. Such people tell me again and again that they come to church to hear my sermons, and, having heard them, can then go on to participate in the liturgy with a sense that the left brain has been nurtured sufficiently to permit the indulgence of the right brain in ritual play. Not a bad bargain.

Thus have these sermons been preached to a congregation in intellectual flux. They are now offered to readers who may themselves be in that flux or who may wish to test the waters of rigorous inquiry. The sermons are not a defense of the faith nor yet proclamations of tenets that are inaccessible to objective testing and analysis. They are attempts to be intellectually honest, to treat congregants as adults, to stimulate thinking and mature consideration of ideas.

While they are presented under copyright, I encourage those fellow preachers who may find them helpful to quote from them at will. Plagiarists, however, will be hunted down relentlessly and ruthlessly exposed.

Abundant thanks is due my intellectual and life's companion, Sue Chevalier, who, besides her criticisms (always constructive) and encouragement (never cheerleading), has edited and designed this book and its cover. She bears me up day and night.

Thanks also to my companions on the way: those in St. Andrew's parish who have studied with me on Monday nights and Wednesday mornings, yea these many years. Their loyalty to the cause of learning has made working in institutional religion more palatable for me.

I fear the church has not often enough been a venue for serious study. Because of that, generations of laity have been defrauded and deprived of the right to worship God with their minds. It is my unflinching purpose to do what I can to redress that grievance.

Finally, I dedicate this book to my teachers over the years without whose patience and tutelage I would not have the wherewithal, sketchy as it may be, to have committed this book. They are: Leonard Clayton Bailey, Joseph James Irwin and George Arthur Buttrick, all of blessed memory, and Paul B. Hessert, Helen Harton Manning and David Lott Strickler.

— Harry T. Cook

How to read this book

This book does not have the usual beginning, middle and end. It is composed of sermons that were given at different times and in different liturgical seasons, reflecting the different conditions and situations among the people to whom they were originally addressed and in the larger world. The sermons, therefore, stand alone individually as singular statements of biblical reflection, theology and teaching.

The reader is invited to pick up the book and to turn to one or another of the sermons and read it at one sitting — none will take more than five minutes. The length of the sermons as they appear herein is deceptive. Written originally for the ear, they now appear in print for the eye. When spoken conversationally during the liturgy, which as a whole lasts about an hour, the sermons last seven to ten minutes.

Moreover, the liturgy, with all its verbal and hymnodic symbolism, was the original setting for these homilies. By themselves, they may seem a bit austere and removed. Imagine them in their native context, and read the scripture referred to at the beginning of each one. That should help set the scene for the sermon itself.

For years I resisted the reprinting of sermons, believing that they live only in the actual interchange of preacher and hearer on the specific occasions they are offered in the context of a congregation's liturgy. Enough trusted friends have clamored for copies of individual sermons, and then for an anthology of them, that I gave in — reluctance intact, but bowing to demand.

My sermons are a labor of intellectual sweat and blood as I grapple with received tradition. I respect that tradition. I was reared and nurtured in it. But the world has largely moved beyond it; so, therefore, must pulpit comment if it is to be useful to people.

Read these sermons as you might the op-ed page columns in a newspaper — not as news themselves but as commentary on the news. As New Testament scholar John Dominic Crossan reminds us, "The gospel is the good news updated."

Part One

Sermons on General Topics

Struggling with the question of God

Exodus 32: 1, 7-14

Maybe the word "God" is just a verbal golden calf. "God" is a word of human invention. But what about the concept behind the word?

Israel's episode with its golden calf, which may not have been as brief as the passage from Exodus depicts it, puts on exhibit a people struggling with the question of God. As we will see, they called that idea by a bewildering variety of names, suggesting perhaps the depth of the confusion of their struggle.

Israel began its life, as near as we can tell, as a wilderness people. We cannot know and can only guess at what they saw, heard, felt or otherwise perceived during that sojourn. But some of the names by which they called that perceived presence among them in nature and history suggest that they perceived it in many and various phenomena.

Nevertheless, human beings generally want concrete, palpable reality on which to hold, so it was not enough to own a deity with whom only a Moses could communicate, and, at that, only upon a cloud-veiled mountaintop. The deity needed to be visible to the eye, touchable to the exploring finger. Hence, the infamous golden calf.

Yet Israel was terribly ambivalent about idol worship, as the Exodus passage implies. Israel came, eventually, to the acknowledgment of one *Yahweh* as the people's conceptualization of a deity. We say "Yahweh," but it is only an approximation of how the name might have been pronounced so long ago. Hebrew was without vowels for a very long time, so that the name for "deity" was the equivalent of our letters Y-H-W-H. In the English of bible study, the name has been rendered as "Jehovah," as "Yahweh," and in numerous variations upon both. As to translation, we who study ancient languages provisionally offer two primary alternative meanings of the name: "I am the one who is present" and "I cause to be what is."

In the wider Semitic world of antiquity, the particle "El" seems to have meant roughly the same. Springing from that came a string of names, all of which apparently denoted what we call "god": El Shadday (god of the mountain), El Olam (god of everlastingness), El Bethel (god of the shrine), Elohim (plural of El), Eloha (perhaps a form of calling out to El), and so on.

Israel was clearly formed and shaped by some kind of economic and political oppression. Numerous texts of case-law jurisprudence in Exodus and Deuteronomy are evidence of this. In any case, it seems clear that Israel did not invent the idea of god out of whole cloth. The people's baffling encounters with mystery caused them to wonder about the ebb and flow of history and nature: "Why does it flood? Why is there drought? Why did that other tribe beat us so badly? Is it something we said or did?" And what Israel perceived seemed to have been a whole that was greater than the sum of its parts.

Into that mix was stirred the people of Israel's exposure to the cultic practices of the peoples and nations among whom from time to time they lived, so that the spare wilderness god of mysterious presence and causative effect became a many-faceted god as much of human invention as not. So the struggle went on.

One of the flaws inherent in almost all contemporary religions is that too few of their adherents struggle with the question of god. The concept is accepted a priori, much as a theorem of geometry: unneedful of further analysis. By such adherents, "god" is spoken of in the masculine, as personal, as accessible as room service in a five-star hotel and able to be manipulated by prayer.

I wonder if our religious initiatives would be taken more seriously by others and by ourselves if we were to engage more honestly and energetically in the struggle to perceive that greater presence and causative effect we presently call "god." And, by the way, we are certainly not required to use the same names for that concept that our Semitic forebears used. We are entitled to come up with new ones that may better suit the intellectual realities of our time. St. John did precisely that in his first epistle written near the end of the first century C.E. in which he boldly declared "God is love," which can just as easily mean "Love is god."

What if for a time we were to put a moratorium on the use of the word "God," and concentrate more intensely on the ebb and flow of history, on the vistas both small and great served up by nature and upon the thoughts and feelings that well up within us unbidden as we try to get a handle on the reality we seek in speaking the name "God"?

Institutional religions and their creeds can sometimes take on the appearance of golden calves. They are the work of human hands but are marketed as divinely ordained and therefore beyond question or analysis.

Maturity in religion is being content with the cloud-veiled ambiguity of a mountaintop, with the unconsumed but nevertheless burning bush, with the still small voice out of nowhere, with the hint or prompting here and there in the warp and woof of nature's and history's progression. Maybe "It" need be called by no particular name, since no name of human invention could possibly account for all that human beings think or believe a god to be capable of being and doing.

In any event, let's avoid the specter of any kind of intellectual golden calf. It's been done already, and, as we have seen, it didn't work.

Out of catastrophe, a vision of glory

Job 19:23-27a

There's no end of trouble, pain and suffering. "Stuff" happens. The key is not to succumb to despair.

What possesses a person to look up from the scene of a personal catastrophe and say, "This doesn't matter because I know I will survive it"? That's exactly what poor old Job is depicted as doing in that brief passage from the book named for him. After all that befell him — one terrible thing after another — he was able, even anxious, to say that, withal, God was on his side and that he would one day see God face-to-face, and not as a stranger.

This reminds me of a couplet I heard somewhere: "Two men looked through prison bars; the one saw mud, the other saw stars." Each of us has felt or will feel that the bottom has dropped out of our lives at one time or another. A spouse, a parent, or, God forbid, a child dies. A career goes down the tube. The job is lost, a home is destroyed, a friendship ruined beyond repair. How do you find any hope or comfort in any of that? Not to do so is to invite the onset of living death.

I heard a man the other day say that he had to pinch himself every morning to make sure he wasn't dreaming. "Life has been so good to me," he said. Not more than five years ago that man was enveloped in despair as his wife, the mother of his children, died that slow, inch-by-inch way which cancer takes. Upon her death, he was the picture of devastation. Today, he says he's on top of the world. How did he get from the death of his wife and the depths to which that took him to the sustained height of his buoyancy today? In the same way old Job picked himself up out of the multiple disasters of his life to proclaim: "I know that my Redeemer liveth, and that he shall stand upon the earth, and my eyes shall behold him and not as a stranger."

That is not Pollyanna speaking. It is no whistling through the proverbial graveyard, no spiritual boosterism. It is realism at its best. Here's what we know. We know that, even after the doomsday bomb exploded over Hiroshima, forever changing the world, the sun rose the next morning as it has every day since, as it did every day before. We know as surely as we know anything that the trees which shed their leaves each fall will by spring produce buds which by Memorial Day will be full leaves. We know that winter is not annihilation. Apparently Job knew those things, too. He was able to marshal the facts at hand and organize them in such a way that they pointed beyond the present to a conceivable future.

At the height of a violent summer storm, I was driving to a hospital to visit a parishioner. I was awash in a downpour. The wind was lashing my car with sheets of rain. But off in the northwest was a brilliant sun preceded by a line of clouds that was the clearing. This, I thought, is what life is like in a dynamic, ever-changing world. Sometimes the world changes too dramatically and too rapidly for us, as a heart simply stops working or an accident snuffs out a life. Or the change comes glacially with the attendant pain and anguish. Either way, it tends to shut down optimism and to make hope a thing of fancy.

The universe seems uncaring of feeling and indiscriminate in its caprice. Jesus observed the same phenomenon but accounted for it in gentler terms: "The rain falls on the just and the unjust." The contemporary bumper sticker says it, too: "Stuff happens." William Faulkner, in accepting the Nobel Prize for literature, gave a remarkable speech in which he observed that mankind (he would say today *human*kind) was destined not only to endure but prevail. Ernest Hemingway once observed that it is essential for the human being to act rather than to be acted upon.

This adds up to a muscular kind of humanism in which human beings individually and collectively discover a sense of power within themselves that mirrors the inexorable forces which make this Earth roll onward into light, which makes a barren tree flower year after year and the grass to turn from a dead brown to a live green after one spring shower.

All of nature calls the entirety of itself to renewal, resurgence, to a kind of here-and-now immortality in which new life springs from the old and the future from the past. We hear often enough a realism to the effect that something will surely get worse before it gets better. And that is just as often true. In those cases, we gird up our loins. Eventually we hit bottom, and there is nowhere to go but up.

That's where we found Job this morning: at the very bottom of the abyss, not looking down but up, toward the source of the shaft of light that was his hope. Job thus stands in our literary history as one who could see a vision of glory beyond the catastrophe. As such, he is or can be our mentor as "stuff happens," leaving us breathless, clueless and potentially hopeless. Yet, as the popular song of 20 years ago put it, "the sun will come up tomorrow." The reality it illuminates is not always pretty, as in the pillow on the other side of the bed where now no beloved head rests or in an empty place at the supper table. But the sun did come up, and it will come up the day after tomorrow and the day after that.

So, hurrah for Job. As St. Paul wrote in a similar vein:

"We are treated as imposters, and yet are true; as unknown, and yet are well known; as dying, and behold we live; as punished, and yet not killed; as sorrowful, yet always rejoicing; as poor, yet making many rich; as having nothing, and yet possessing everything."

The problem of wealth

Luke 16:1-13

Having money can be as much of a problem as not having money ... if you take the gospel seriously.

So you see that the subject of this sermon is "The problem of wealth." You think immediately of the imminent mortgage payment, the next installment of your kid's college tuition or your little stock investment on its Wall Street roller coaster, and you say, "That's one problem I don't have. I'm not wealthy." Yes and no.

There's an Episcopal church not 15 minutes drive from here where wealth might actually be a problem, for it is a parish, not only of the well-to-do but of the very well-to-do. So, you would say, they're wealthy.

On the other hand, there is an Episcopal church perhaps 30 minutes from here on the near east side of Detroit where we would be thought of as fabulously wealthy. The concept of wealth, therefore, is relative.

What does it mean to be wealthy? Could it be something so simple as a state of mind? A friend tells of a long-ago Christmas when her husband was between jobs — and not on purpose, either. They had no money to buy the usual round of gifts, so they made little things together, baked cookies and essentially gave of themselves. The friend says it was the best Christmas the family ever had. "We felt we were rich," she says. So maybe wealth is more than one's financial worth. Maybe it is a state of mind.

Those of us who stand in the pulpit are frequently accused of "always preaching about money" as if money were a bad word. Maybe it is, but if so, be on notice that it is quite often the topic of moment in many places in the Bible, including today's gospel.

The passage is a jumble of images and seeming contradictions, but it all has to do with money, as we have heard — a rich man, his inept property manager reducing the obligations of the rich man's debtors so as to curry favor; the rich man's curious comment "make friends for yourselves by means of dishonest wealth so that when it is gone, they may welcome you into the eternal homes"; and finally the familiar remonstrance to the effect that one has, in the end, to choose between God and wealth.

Money in whatever quantity is not in itself a problem. It's one's attitude toward it and about it. John D. Rockefeller used to tip Pullman porters a dime when the standard tip was a quarter. But Rockefeller gave millions of dollars away. He built an entire university, the University of Chicago. For his day and age, he lived modestly. He famously said he owned only one pair of shoes at a time because he could wear only one ... at a time. The Rockefeller Foundation has done enormous good throughout the world in this century.

So it's how one thinks of money that is the crux of the issue. The gospel tells us that to equate one's highest loyalty with money is an invitation to disaster. OK, then, how rich are you? Not as rich as some, not so poor as others? Most would rather have more.

I don't know of anyone who wants less. A good number — and I would put myself among them — are satisfied with what they have.

Unlike John D. Rockefeller, I own more than one pair of shoes. I also have some money left over each month after I pay the bills, pay my church pledge and buy the groceries. It's what I do with that remainder that makes the difference. I could sock it all away in the bank and let the interest compound. I could simply spend it on whatever pleases me. Either of those choices would mark me as a wealthy individual, because wealth is a relative thing. It is relative to one's life circumstances. And were I to use my relative wealth entirely in a selfish manner, caring more about myself and my desires, I would be basically worshiping money rather than some higher, loftier loyalty or value. And that would be a problem. In light of the scriptures it would, in fact, be immoral.

I'm not sure how this fits in, but it comes to mind in this discussion. Last year, the big planes of Northwest Airlines were grounded when its pilots went on strike to protest the stinginess of management. The pilots and other Northwest employees had agreed to big wage concessions five years before, when the airline was near bankruptcy. With a return to enormous profitability, management decided to keep the windfall to themselves. According to the New York Times, Northwest's CEO sold 300,000 shares of the company's stock (obtained on a discount option) for $19 million. That's on top of the CEO's six-figure salary. And the guy couldn't fly even a paper airplane. No man can serve two masters. You cannot serve the interests of money and the interests of humanity at the same time.

OK, so perhaps you and I don't have $19 million in stock options. But we're not down-and-out, either. We're far more fortunate than the needy souls fed and cared for by the local homeless shelter. Wealth is a relative thing. What we do with the extra is the measure of our humanity.

Are you convinced — and by what?

Luke 16:19-31

Doing justice is not rocket science. Anybody can be a doer, a bringer of justice. The directions are all in The Book.

One of the chief criticisms of my book *Christianity Beyond Creeds,* as well as of a number of my sermons, is that I have cast doubt on the proposition that Jesus was physically resurrected. I thought both of that proposition and the criticism when I read Luke's parable of the rich man and the poor beggar, Lazarus.

The rich man sees in his extremity the errors of omission caused by his ignorance (or disregard?) of Lazarus' plight, and the dire consequences of his ignorance. He is eternally sunk in a ditch, but he has five brothers yet living and does not wish upon them his misery, so he asks Abraham to dispatch a resurrected Lazarus to the brothers as a warning, that they may be spared this torture. Abraham replies that all they need do is pay attention to the scriptures of their religion, and all will be well. The rich man disagrees. Something astonishing is required. Abraham's laconic last word on the subject is: "If they do not listen to Moses and the prophets, neither will they be convinced even if someone rises from the dead."

Convinced of what? That it is absolutely necessary to tend systemically and consistently to the needs and requirements of the disadvantaged — or take the consequences.

I have found to my amazement how absolutely convinced so very many people are that Jesus was raised from the dead and that, therefore, they may be, too, if they mind their p's and q's. Are you so convinced?

Moses and the prophets, meaning the Law and the Prophets, are supposed to be the agents of our conviction — if I'm reading this text correctly. It's all there in black-and-white. Here are samples: "Let justice roll down like waters and righteousness as an everlasting stream." (Amos) "You shall not oppress the alien. The alien shall be to you as the citizen among you; you shall love him as yourself." (Leviticus) "Is this not the fast I choose, to loose the bonds of injustice, to undo the thongs of the yoke, to let the oppressed go free?" (Isaiah). Of that we are to be convinced.

The dictionary at my desk says that the meaning of the phrase "to be convinced" comes from the Latin "vincere": to conquer or to be conquered by. Moses and the prophets are to be, in effect, our conquerors so that, with all our defenses dismantled, we are faced with an undeniable and enormous truth. And that truth seems to be that under God's rule there are to be no rich people and no poor beggars. There are to be persons in community so that, as Moses also says, "those who have much do not have too much, and those who have little do not have too little." Not a strictly arithmetic socialist equality, but a fundamental and decent fairness.

That is a truth of which Luke's legendary rich

man was clearly not convinced. Luke does not say that he was a bad person who deliberately oppressed the poor. The time in which Luke lived was anything but an era of equality. There were an oligarchy of the rich and a majority of peasants on the borderline between poverty and destitution. That's how it was. The appearance of Jesus on the public stage with his subversive denunciations of the situation made him at first a bizarre curiosity and, as time went along, evidently a seditious threat to the status quo.

Luke's parable of the rich man and the unseen beggar at his gate is a graphic and dramatic extension of Jesus' economic program. The terms of the parable are, of course, highly theatrical and are not meant to be taken literally. Obviously, the departed do not have conversations with likewise dead Hebrew patriarchs, and a just god cannot be conceived of as an agent of eternal torture. What, then, can we extract by way of meaning from this parable?

I suggest that its core meaning may be that there are natural and sometimes unavoidable consequences of both action and inaction, of both cognizance and ignorance — or a combination of them. One who is cognizant of the beggar at the gate and keeps him in beggary may be courting a revolution. Nicholas II, Mother Russia's last czar, learned that lesson the hard way. One who becomes cognizant of the beggar and works to make him self-sufficient may be in the position of having less himself when the newly enfranchised ex-beggar has more in a world of limited resources.

One who is not cognizant of the beggar and therefore lulled into thinking he doesn't exist will know the consequences of ignorance only at the moment they tumble upon him like a load of bricks. Or perhaps upon his children or grandchildren, because the sins of the father are often enough visited upon their progeny in a world in which, as they say, stuff happens.

This is the alarm bell in the night that has been sounded now for 30 years by Detroit's Focus: HOPE and like initiatives in which the desperately poor and unemployable are being gathered up and equipped and empowered to self-sufficiency, thus reducing the number of beggars at the gate — to use Luke's stark and unpleasant figure of speech. Our own Episcopal

Church's Funds for Economic Justice is on a parallel course — not in running soup kitchens and shelters, but in trying to create an economic and therefore political environment in which there will be far less need for such temporary, stopgap programs.

The consequences of not doing so can range anywhere from riot and insurrection to an eventual and abysmal disappointment on the part of those who had and could but didn't.

Are you convinced?

The inevitability of division

Luke 12:49-56

Agreeing to disagree in charity about deeply held convictions is about the only way to keep the peace!

"Do you think that I have come to bring peace to the earth? No, I tell you, but rather division," said Jesus. This is not a happy text. It speaks of division and discord among people who should be happy together, *i.e.*, the family that is the church. This is the same Jesus who, Luke says 11 chapters earlier, has come to bring "peace, good will among men." Which is it? How can it be both? How could the supposed agent of God's peace become the agent of division and discord?

Part of what surely persuaded and persuades our

Jewish sisters and brothers that Jesus of Nazareth was not and is not the messiah is that he did not bring in the reign of "shalom," of peace and good will. In fact, the effect of his appearance on the public scene was the antithesis of peace. It brought conflict, and it seems to have been purposeful — so Jesus is depicted as having said.

For all its fervid prayers and aspiration for unity, the consistent mark of the church, lo these two millennia, has been division. For example:

- the several centuries of controversy over what was orthodoxy and what was heresy;
- the papal intrigues of the 14th century which featured murder, poisoning and other dark arts;
- the estrangement and bitterness of the Reformation and Counter-Reformation;
- the brutal theocracy of John Calvin's Geneva;
- the crazy quilt of American Protestantism and the specter of Protestants protesting other Protestants;
- the division of churches over abolition versus slavery;
- the fracturing of church relationships over civil

rights, the Vietnam War, the ordination of women and the acceptance of gay and lesbian persons.

Meanwhile, the Prayer Book includes several well-loved and much-used prayers for unity. Their inclusion and use may reflect the maxim of St. Thomas Aquinas to the effect that “it is legitimate to pray for that which it is legitimate to desire.” And yet in a dynamic and prophetic religion, division seems inevitable. It is part of the deal; it is, like the poor, always to be with us. The issue is how to deal with division.

Martin Luther dealt with it by declaring, “Ich kann nicht anders,” which translates to “I can do no other” — in other words, “I’ve got to do what I’ve got to do.” Rome dealt with Luther by excommunicating him. Calvin dealt with division by burning Servetus at the stake. I would say that neither of those examples is helpful.

What I have learned — and learned the hard way — is that relationships are of greater importance than ideas. We are called into community; why, we know not. No community of any kind anywhere can avoid periodic division and discord. It’s like what physicists describe as the natural disorder in the universe. A couple who experiences discord deals with it by continuing to love one another while working things out. Estranged parents and children do it. Races, peoples and nations do it.

The fact remains, though, that Jesus divides us because his ethic is so uncompromising and demanding. Doctrine divides us because it does not proceed from revelation but reason, and we're all in different places intellectually.

One person suggests that it's not the fact of disagreement or division that is the issue, but how the community manages it. We manage it by never walking away from the conversation, by never leaving the table, which is why the culmination of our time together on Sundays is at the holy table from which we share the bread and cup. It may sometimes be the only visible unity we have. But a better unity we could not have.

Faithfully bring forth justice

Isaiah 42:1-9

Religion that counts and that will endure will be expressed in the effecting of justice. Religion for religion's sake is irrelevant.

Of that poetic figure, the suffering servant, a sixth-century B.C.E. Hebrew philosopher named Isaiah said, "He will not grow faint or be crushed until he has established justice in the earth." The so-called suffering servant was for that philosopher of old the embodiment of his people's purpose, their reason for being — namely to bring by and through their corporate life a measure of lasting justice to the world. How a smallish people could bear such a lofty expectation is one of the remarkable images of the Bible.

One can see in the amazing life of the Jewish people how, on the one hand, they have suffered and, on the other, they have by that suffering effected justice. The Holocaust of the 20th century — one of its most horrible scars — surely helped fuel the American civil rights movement and the various humanitarian undertakings of the United Nations. Genocide became a punishable crime, thanks to the Holocaust, as the butchers of Serbia, Rwanda and Burundi may eventually appreciate.

It may be that such people as the Palestinians — Muslim and Christian — are the suffering servants of our time, whose suffering and claims for justice may yet effect it, with the entire human race benefiting.

Meanwhile, the Christian religion has long since appropriated the image of the suffering servant as a metaphor for Jesus seeking to understand his execution in the light of vicarious suffering, namely that Jesus' suffering somehow spared our own. On balance, that is a rather primitive interpretation which we do well to avoid in these days. But if you understand that Jesus' teachings and what the gospels portray of his life are what even indirectly led him to the cross, then we might credibly say at the end of the 20th century that he is (or was) a suffering servant in the mold of Isaiah's vision.

Even a cursory examination of any of the two or three dozen sayings reasonably attributed to Jesus of Nazareth reveals a person centered on justice — economic or otherwise — for all, based on the concept of worth and dignity of the individual. It is perhaps an open question as to whether Jesus grew faint, to use Isaiah's words, or was crushed before he established justice on the Earth. One way the church has attempted to deal with that question has been its proclamation of the resurrection. Maybe Jesus was down, but he was not out.

Somehow, though, the proclamation of the resurrection got turned into a vehicle of personal, individual salvation, as in: If you believe Jesus was raised from the dead, then so will you be. That's the wrong emphasis altogether. If you're going to proclaim his resurrection, you need to proclaim it as a vindication of his teachings about human worth and justice.

If you're going to proclaim the resurrection, do so as a pretext of a program of justice, as in: It may fly in the face of Wall Street's mantra of free-market capitalism, but it is nonetheless right and proper to distribute wealth in equitable and just ways; it is right to put down the mighty from their thrones and to exalt the humble and meek; it is right to lift up the valleys, and make the mountains low, the uneven ground level and the rough places plain.

Those who attempt to effect such ends are likely to suffer for it. When the Episcopal Church, at the bidding of its then-Presiding Bishop John Elbridge Hines, turned its attention to the inner cities of this country in the wake of the riots of the mid-1960s, it lost membership and resources. Corporately, it suffered. But in its suffering it effected justice by being a model of its effecting. It is the church I fell in love with.

The more a congregation moves from maintenance to mission, from marking time to marching on, from doing the usual to doing justice, the more it will appear to be the resurrected Jesus instead of an embalmed corpse.

We're here faithfully to execute justice, and we are not to faint or allow ourselves to be crushed before we do it.

Come and see

John 1:29-41

"What would Jesus do?" That seems to be a question a great many people are asking. One answer is that whatever he might do, he would not be doing it in a church.

Sometimes the Bible speaks with a spare economy of words. That is the case in the text from the Gospel of John in which disciples of John the Baptist are depicted as asking Jesus where he was staying. Jesus' reply was: "Come and see." Where was it? The gospel writer never says. The answer is left to us to figure out. The Jesus of the gospels doesn't tell us where he stays; he invites us to come and see.

During a trip to Italy, my family and I saw the

inside of plenty of churches, cathedrals, shrines and basilicas. Yes, they were beautiful; some are awe-inspiring. No expense was spared to make them so. They are each in their own way dedicated to Jesus or to his mother. But I do not think Jesus was in any one of them.

We visited St. Peter's Church, the seat of Roman Catholicism, and walked within a yard or less of the tombs of popes. We stood at the foot of the papal altar. A choir was chanting mass nearby. Incense was in the air. But I do not think Jesus was there.

Nearby was the Sistine Chapel, where Michelangelo's monumental frescoes tell biblical stories in a breathtaking sweep of the artist's brush. There, for centuries, consistories of cardinals have solemnly elected popes. Everywhere is a sense of sanctity. But I do not think Jesus was there.

After we finished the obligatory tour of the Duomo, the massive cathedral of Florence, we visited the museum workshop across the narrow lane where Michelangelo is said to have worked and which houses several dozen pieces of matchless objects of art. It did not occur to me to think that Jesus was there, either — until I turned a corner and saw before me a life-size bronze sculpture by the Renaissance artist Donatello. Though it was given a title printed on a small card attached to the pedestal, I did not have to look at the card. I knew who the figure was. It was La Madellena — Mary Magdalene.

How Donatello had managed to convey in bronze the unkempt and stringy hair, the almost toothless mouth and the ragged dress, I cannot say. But there she was: frozen in midstep, a look of urgent entreaty from begging eyes and lips apart as if to utter a supplication. You know that invisible before her was Jesus, who had come to stay where she was, who had come to befriend and succor her.

For the first and only time in two weeks in a country where churches are at every turn, I knew where Jesus was. And as I stood in that museum workshop, my cheeks wet with tears, the words of the hymn came to mind:

Where cross the crowded ways of life,
where sound the cries of race and clan,

above the noise of selfish strife,
we hear thy voice, O Son of Man.

In haunts of wretchedness and need,
on shadowed thresholds dark with tears,
from paths where hide the lures of greed,
we catch the vision of thy tears.

O Master from the mountainside
make haste to heal these hearts of pain;
among these restless throngs abide,
O tread the city's streets again.

Where is Jesus staying? Come and see. Come and see, for example, the works of the Diocese of Michigan's H. Coleman McGehee Funds for Economic Justice as they redistribute wealth and enable the poor and disenfranchised to help themselves, thus fulfilling the baptismal covenant that commits us to respect the dignity of every human being.

It is to the McGehee Funds for Economic Justice that St. Andrew's consigns a gift made to our parish in memory of one of the church's most distinguished servants.

Jesus is staying where this gift is going. Come and see.

Heart's desire

Psalm 37:4

If you're looking for God, try looking into the eyes of the person next to you — and as you do so, remember Jesus' famous answer to the question, "Who is my neighbor?"

"Take delight in the Lord," the psalmist wrote, "and he shall give you your heart's desire." Who doesn't want his or her heart's desire? But who knows what it means to "take delight in the Lord," when there are so many other more obvious and material things in which to take delight — and with more immediate gratification?

What would be your heart's desire, and would you conceive of finding it in taking delight in God?

In some circles, the mere mention of the Anglo-Saxon word "God" can shut down the most congenial of social occasions. In others, though, "God" (the word) is almost obligatory, as in: "I turned my life over to God, and, see, all is well." How very differently do people use the word "God." For some, it conjures up perceived abuses or offenses from youthful years. For others, it is a comfort word that has the effect of a cup of marshmallow-festooned hot chocolate. So before one can decide to "take delight in the Lord," we'd better agree on what "the Lord" is.

From a rational perspective, the term "Lord" is a verbal symbol for the perceived connection between ourselves and the rest of the universe. Both instinct and common sense tell us that we are effects of a higher power. The presence in us of individual and collective consciences strongly suggests that such a higher power has a moral core and moral expectations of the universe, or at least those parts of it that possess a conscience. Order and harmony are clearly desirable characteristics of morality, as in, for example, when we treat others as we wish to be treated.

To take delight in that is to win the heart's desire which is surely to live in security, reasonably good health and in the self-realization of purpose and accomplishment.

You can't live in that way if you and the other abide in mutual fear and distrust, if you poison the air you breathe and the water you drink. So what you want and how you want to live are quite dependent upon how you relate to the other and to the world. "Taking delight in the Lord," then, is insofar as possible to be in harmony with one's world and one's neighbors in it.

Some will say, "But what about God? What about 'spirituality'?" My answer to such questions is a big, "I don't know." I keep stumbling over the arresting wisdom of I John 4:20: "Those who say, 'I love God,' and hate their brothers and sisters, are liars; for those who do not love a brother or sister whom they can see, cannot love God whom they cannot see."

More horrendous crimes against humanity have been committed in the name of God than I care to enumerate. More zealots claiming love for Vishnu,

Jaweh and Allah have slaughtered more innocents than history dares record.

I think the correct way to express the Great Commandant is this: "You shall love the Lord your God with all your heart, soul, mind and strength by loving your neighbor as yourself." One who claimed to be James the Brother of Jesus wrote: "What good is it if you say you have faith but do not back it up with works? If a brother or sister lacks daily food and you tell them, 'Go in peace and eat your fill' yet do nothing to supply their need, what is the good of that? Faith without works is dead."

It's easier, of course, to concentrate one's religious efforts on an unseen god than on utterly visible fellow human beings, because one unseen and unheard is likely not to make a person accountable, save to his own fancy. Therefore, the religion that survives into the 21st century — that is, survives to be effective and to be taken seriously — will be one in which the heart's desire is for harmony and peace with the biosphere and one's fellow beings, and in which the fulfillment of that desire is sought in the doing of good works for the sake of doing them, for the joy of doing them to, for and with the other.

The eighth century B.C.E. Hebrew commentator Micah posed the question of what the Lord requires of those who would acknowledge him. Micah's answer was, "To do justice, to love kindness and thereby to walk humbly with God."

And there you have it.

Pass the salt

Matthew 5:13-20

Winston S. Churchill once said of a dessert that had been set before him: "Pray, remove this pudding. It has no theme." What would he say about contemporary Christianity?

"You are the salt of the earth" is what Jesus told the people who were curious about him, people who were following or thinking of following him. "You are the salt of the earth."

In all of human history, salt has had two main purposes: to preserve and to enhance. In these latter days, salt is sometimes a no-no for those with hypertension. Thus as with most blessings, salt has a downside. Yet its positive properties are beneficial. A stalk of celery by itself is a study in blandness. But with a dash of salt, it is to some the food of the gods. I will push a bowl of oatmeal away if I am not permitted to salt it. Salt has the property to enhance healthy but bland food.

Salt also preserves. That is less an issue for us in late 20th-century civilization in which refrigeration is now commonplace. But when and where it has not been, salt has done the job. Salt will preserve meat in particular and keep it desirably edible for quite a long time. Road salt, of course, makes winter's way easier in all the ways we know. Salt — the iodized form — is protection against serious glandular disease.

Salt preserves and enhances. Jesus knew that even as he called those he hoped would buy and live out his message "the salt of the earth." What did he mean?

Certainly there were things to preserve. Jesus, while critical of excesses and omissions by some practitioners of his tradition, nevertheless saw the Judaism of his time worthy and needful of preservation. He is said to have told the same people he called "the salt of the earth" that he had come not to abolish the law and the prophets but to fulfill them, and that none of it would pass away until their every jot and tittle was observed. And he was telling those who would follow him that they should be the agents of its preservation. And they were: They remembered and set down his own words on the subject and passed on his ethical wisdom about how people can live together in usefulness and peace.

But just as clearly, Jesus saw that his tradition had grown listless and unappealing, if not sometimes downright counterproductive. It was out of that conviction that he shocked his world by suggesting that the sabbath tradition was made for human beings — for their rest, fulfillment and self-realization — not human beings for the sabbath, that is for its rigid and burdensome observance.

Here and now, you and I are not interested in the immediate question of sabbath observance but in that of which it is a symptom. The problem of keeping that which is meant to serve from becoming that which must be served is a universal one.

Governments that are meant to serve their people easily become their tyrant governors. Religions which are clearly the products of the highest human effort and aspiration become the agents of human oppression. Institutions and corporations almost always become hierarchical in nature and thus, inevitably, weigh upon those lower down the pecking order with orders, commands and threats.

That's what Jesus saw in his day, and he announced himself opposed to it. In his "salt of the earth" statement, I think he was calling upon the best in his Jewish tradition — the socially conscious, justice-driven prophets — and summoning his contemporaries to enhance their religion, to season it with the bite and zing of the prophetic wisdom. I think he was hoping that the salt had not lost its savor, had not lost its power to enhance and to make a difference.

No less are Jesus' followers today to be the preserving and enhancing element of both church and society. No less are they — are we — to discover in ourselves and our religion that seasoning of justice and mercy which can reform and transform a culture whose institutions have become oppressive and denying of human dignity.

Does that amount to mixing religion and politics? Only in the sense that a dash of salt can make the difference between a mess of pottage and a delectable stew.

Those who would identify themselves as followers of Jesus are, then, like the salt shaker on the table, quite totally differentiated in substance and purpose from the various foods upon the table, but with the power to bring out the best in them. Is it any wonder that technology has found it profitable to develop and market salt substitutes?

The lesson is that if the real salt loses its savor, a substitute will be found for it. How do you think that reality applies to the church as we know it?

John 3:16?

John 3:1-17

Going to heaven is not, after all, the chief end of the practice of religion. And "eternal life" doesn't mean living forever.

You've seen it: a large piece of cloth or canvas draped over a stadium rail during a major athletic event — say the Super Bowl. And on that cloth or canvas appears in big block letters the legend: JOHN 3:16. You've seen it also on bumper stickers, lawn signs and outdoor church bulletin boards.

"For God so loved the world that he gave his only son, that whoever believes in him should not perish but have eternal life." Longtime Episcopalians will remember this verse as one of the so-called Comfortable Words which occurred in the communion service after the Confession and Absolution.

What about this verse compels people to make it into a slogan? I asked that question of a colleague whose response was, "It's the cheapest and ultimate life insurance. If you can convince a person that by summoning belief in Jesus — whatever that might mean — he or she can be guaranteed eternal life — whatever *that* might mean — then you have sold that person an unbeatable policy. It's a wonder Christianity doesn't sell it at a premium."

It is a wonder, and, of course, the pre-Reformation Catholic Church tried something very like it in its sale of indulgences — or time out of purgatory. Luther's thunderous 95 theses spelled the end of all that. But the underlying fear of the popularity of the indulgence persists. A recent poll revealed that more than 78 percent of Americans are concerned about what will happen to them after they die. (Why does no pollster ask me?) The popularity of the promise of John 3:16 is thus explained. So the questions the rational person must ask about it are:

1) What does it mean to believe in Jesus?

2) What does the verb "to perish" mean?

3) What is "eternal life"?

I do honestly and accurately say that I believe in Susan Chevalier, the woman to whom I am married now for 20 years. Of course, I believe that she exists. So, I suppose, do you. But across the 20 years that we have shared love and life, I have come to believe in her — in her extraordinary capabilities, in her unerring sense of what works, in her skills and integrity as a parent. In short, I have placed my life and my future in her hands. I make no significant choices or decisions without her and covet every minute in her presence. I am governed by our covenant as wife and husband; her approval is the pearl of great price.

It is not possible, and certainly not rational, to believe in a person one cannot see or with whom one cannot converse. The closest I can get to believing in Jesus is to act on his basic ethical principles centered on the Golden Rule. If I base my life — bet my life — on that rule, it could be said that I believe in Jesus.

That, of course, is not good enough for some. I

have in my files the most extraordinary letter of its kind I have ever read. It is from a member of this congregation in which he resigned from the parish because his rector would not preach the necessity of what the writer called "the blood atonement of Jesus Christ for human sin." That's what the letter writer meant by believing in Jesus — believing that Jesus died for his sins. And apart from such belief, he would perish. (Maybe I'm in the wrong business.)

What can the term "to perish" mean? To my friend, the letter writer, perishing meant just that: a fiery and eternal damnation in a Dante-esque hell — all because the damned could not or would not believe in the blood atonement. My final words (at least to date) with that man were to this effect: "Joe, if that is your vision of a just and merciful god, you'd be better off an atheist."

Here's what the term "to perish" may mean in the arena of rational religion: an entire world laid waste as the lives of ethnic Albanians in Kosovo are laid waste by the most brutal forms of human hate; a planet increasingly despoiled by ignorant, selfish, shortsighted human beings; a global economy increasingly tilted in favor of the wealthy at the expense of the disadvantaged.

Which brings us to what the idea of "eternal life" can mean to rational folk. Virtually everything we know about the biosphere strongly suggests that there is no such thing as eternal life as the term is commonly understood. (In the New Testament, the term usually means the life of the kingdom inaugurated by Jesus.) On the other hand, last summer's maple leaf is now in microscopic bits and pieces, part of the rich seed bed of future maples. If we only would, we could appreciate the same basic fact about all biospheric life, including our own.

Eternal life is one of those uniquely human ideas. The basic animal instinct is for survival in the present. Somewhere along the evolutionary line — perhaps as life got better and less brutish for Homo sapiens — the idea arose that it ought to be ever ongoing, especially for good people. I leave to the historians of human psychology the riddle of how belief in such a thing became in the minds of some a ticket to eternal life.

The rational construction of John 3:16 can be expressed in this way:

The creator of the world cared enough for its creatures that its own moral imperative was built into the evolutionary process so that people like Jesus would emerge as great ethical exemplars, and that those who could be moved to live their lives on the basis of such an ethic would effect such a life on this planet as to make anyone living it wish it might be eternal.

Sad to say, such a construction will never satisfy the likes of my onetime parishioner, Joe.

Authority

Luke 4:21-32

Those who traffic in the unvarnished truth about things have more real authority than any dictator, general or admiral. That's why they sometimes meet untimely ends.

Thomas Wolfe's novel-length aphorism, "You Can't Go Home Again," might be a summary of the story that depicts Jesus' homecoming to the synagogue in Nazareth. He did not receive a Chamber of Commerce "local boy makes good" kind of welcome. Had that been in the cards, it was forgone by the flash of his anger at the surprise of his contemporaries over his profundity and clarity of purpose.

The way Luke tells the story, there was plenty of

resentment on the Nazarenes' part because Jesus bristled at their suggestion that he was only a good old boy. What, therefore, would he know? When, in anger, Jesus compared them to Jews of other times who just couldn't get it when the great unwashed pagans did, the fat was in the fire, and lynching was a pregnant possibility.

The Nazarenes, it is said, were astounded and obviously not pleased that Jesus seemed to speak with "exousia," i.e., with the freedom knowing oneself affords. Why is it that those who possess or are possessed by such authority are resented and often silenced? Lincoln, Gandhi and King come to mind.

What constitutes such authority? Four things:

1) the ability and willingness to rationalize and analyze experience rather than merely be driven blindly by it;

2) knowledge;

3) discipline, and

4) courage.

The recollection and rational analysis of one's experience — what Coleridge described poetically as "emotion recollected in tranquillity" — is what makes humans human. It is one thing to have things happen to you. It is quite another to figure out why and how to keep bad things from happening to you again.

Acquiring a broad base of knowledge deep enough to give one insight is a must if one is to be possessed of an inner force. Such knowledge is acquired primarily through discriminating reading of the classics, of history and literature in which great minds have illuminated the human situation. The mind-numbing, miserable content of most television and the barbaric yawp of talk radio are empty fountains.

One acquires knowledge through discipline. There is no shortcut. You begin with the ancient Greek philosophers and work your way through a lifetime to the 20th-century greats, of whom there are a few. What one discovers in doing such reading is that those great works were not written for some scholastic elite. They were written for the "demos" — "the people," as in democracy. St. John was right to put these words on Jesus' lips: "You shall know the truth, and the truth will make you free."

None of this — reflection on experience, the acquisition of knowledge and the discipline entailed in its acquiring — will matter unless one derives courage from it all. I suspect that the deeper one's knowledge is, the broader one's interests, the stricter one's discipline, the stauncher will be one's courage. What is courage?

Courage is the asserted ability to look reality in the face and accept it, not passively, but aggressively to deal with it. William Faulkner in his speech accepting the Nobel Prize for literature said of humankind that "he shall not only endure but prevail."

Courage is knowing who you are and what you know. It is accepting reality rather than denying it and inventing false realities that, in their unreality, are more tolerable and pleasant. How often and how much both politicians and clergy practice that intellectual deception. Politicians tell us what they think we want to hear, i.e., that global warming is just an eccentric notion of tree huggers, that lower taxes and less government spell freedom, that gasoline priced at less than $1 a gallon is one of Jefferson's inalienable rights.

Clergy repeat and attempt to improve upon myths and preach them as reality as a kind of spiritual opiate. No wonder politicians and clergy are no longer thought of as true authority figures.

What impressed and offended the burghers of Nazareth about Jesus was that he knew, that he knew himself, that he was disciplined and courageous to the point of speaking the tabooed truth of things. They hated him for it, and he died in the cause of it. Yet today, Jesus is remembered and celebrated. His executioners are ciphers in the dustbin of history. Few remember the name of Gandhi's assassin. John Wilkes Booth and James Earl Ray are perennially condemned.

The kind of immortality in which Jesus of Nazareth abides is most often attained in the crucible of suffering. So be it. It is what Faulkner meant when he said humankind would "not only endure but prevail." Only authority earned and exercised through thick and through thin can confer such immortality.

Seeing Jesus at the table

Luke 24:13-35

One way for rational Christians to embrace the resurrection in late 20th century terms is to understand that Jesus is present in story, proclamation and conversation as well as in common prayer.

Our familiar gospel story this morning — the Road to Emmaus — comes to us from a late first century perspective, as the ranks of what I call "Jesus Jews" were being sorely tested in the crucible of persecution both by Rome and orthodox synagogue Jews. Already there was disillusionment because a supposedly resurrected Jesus failed to come again in glory as many — including the pre-eminent apostle, Paul of Tarsus — had confidently predicted.

It was during this period that the gospels as we know them first made their appearance — efforts to recover some semblance of memory of the one whose words and demeanor had caused some synagogue Jews to become Jesus Jews. At least one and part of another generation were living with second, third and fourth-hand information about Jesus. He wasn't physically present, and he hadn't come again. Faith was understandably flagging. Into this breach with the lore stepped Mark, Matthew, Luke and John — first century Jesus Jews (or in some cases, perhaps, converts to Jesus Judaism from the Gentile world). Suddenly, if only through story and proclamation, Jesus was once again present. Perhaps one of the most convincing stories is this one: the Road to Emmaus. It is tempting to take this story as literal reportage.

But Luke gives us two rather broad clues that it is not meant to be so taken. The clues are 1) the sudden appearance of the mysterious traveler out of nowhere, and 2) the just as sudden disappearance into the ether of that traveler who turned out to be Jesus once he was recognized. So if the story is not to be taken literally, how shall it be taken?

Other clues: Jesus was present in a way as Cleopas and the other, unnamed disciple were walking along the road together. Jesus was present in their conversation as Luke put it, "about all these things that had happened." And Jesus was present in yet another way as Cleopas and friend sat at table flabbergasted that Jesus had actually, personally been with them over the meal. Luke depicts their converse in this way: "Were not our hearts burning within us while he was talking to us on the road...?" And Jesus remained present in yet another way as Cleopas and friend returned to Jerusalem and "told what had happened on the road, and how he had been made known to them in the breaking of the bread." At no time throughout the story was Jesus ever absent from them. He was present in various ways. That about described things in the late first century, and it describes them now.

We can always find Jesus in our fellowship when we seek and serve him in all people, loving our neighbors as ourselves.

We can always find Jesus in our study, conversations and discussions — in our outreach work in which we seek his face in the face of the poor and homeless.

We can always meet Jesus at the table as we come together with our friends and neighbors to eat pancakes at a parish breakfast, to receive the bread we call his body and the wine we call his blood.

But more to the point as we go out the church doors on Sunday and into our everyday lives, we can meet Jesus as we tell others how important he and his teachings are to us, how they give to life a charitable, generous and peace-making quality.

No one needs to seek Jesus. He is already here, if not in one way then in another.

Part Two

Sermons for special occasions

BAPTISM

How to miss the point

John 9:1-38

Baptism and its aftermath represent an opportunity for a person to learn to see the world through the eyes of Jesus. The church's teaching ministry can provide corrective lenses to the inwardly blind.

You know, of course, the story of the visitor to a very proper Episcopal church. The visitor sang the hymns with gusto, loudly "Amen"-ed the rector's sermon and prayed aloud during the silences. Finally, a well-meaning usher approached her with the request to be more circumspect in her behavior. Her loud reply was, "But I'm getting religion here." The usher responded by saying, "I'm sorry, ma'am, but you can't get religion in the Episcopal Church."

That's a classic lesson in how to miss the point.

Now ordinarily you'd think that a blind person suddenly receiving sight would be big news and a cause for celebration. How it happened would not be nearly as important as the fact that it did happen. That simply isn't the case in this gospel text. Jesus' detractors were frustrated that he was apparently able to effect the sighting of the blind fellow to the degree that they expelled him and his family from the fellowship of the synagogue. Talk about missing the point!

The story probably reflects an actual historical situation from the late first century as tension built between established Judaism and the emerging movement which would later be known as Christianity. Those Jews who saw things as Jesus had seen them were persona non grata with those who did not.

When a congregation welcomes into its midst by baptism a brand-new Christian, his or her parents and sponsors are asked to promise for the newly baptized person that she will seek and serve Jesus in all people, loving her neighbor as herself, and to strive for justice and peace among all people and to respect the dignity of every human being. To do any of that requires that the doer be able to see the world in a radically different light than is customary for human beings. The person who makes such promises or for whom such promises are made will, in effect, have to see things as Jesus saw them.

When Jesus saw a stranger, someone different from he, he saw a potential friend — not a potential enemy. When he saw a handicapped person, he did not recoil. He embraced him as a sister or brother. When Jesus saw one outcast by society, he saw him or her as one to be included. For Jesus, there were no lepers. A lot of people who knew or know about Jesus were and are evidently not keen on his visions of things. To some, the stranger will always be a threat, the visitor who is "getting religion" will be a nuisance, the one whose life orientation may be different will be subject to marginalizing, devaluing, discounting and demonizing.

The sight and vision the fellowship of Jesus intends to have and to share is that wider, deeper vision which sees beyond the obvious, behind the surface, and straight to the heart of the fellow human being — beyond race, class, sexual orientation and station in life.

When the baptismal rite says "to strive for justice and peace, and to respect the dignity of every human being," it means exactly that. Not just some human beings, not just human beings who fit certain categories or demographics, but every human being because he or she is a human being.

That requires a kind of inner 20/20 vision which most of us don't have. That's what church and Sunday school and adult education are about. Such ongoing experience and participation are like corrective lenses. The gospel is a prescription for the sight and vision of Jesus. The cost to get that prescription filled is referenced in the baptismal promises: "Will you continue in the apostle's teaching and fellowship, in the breaking of bread, and in the prayers?"

All those in favor of improved and enhanced sight say, "I will, with God's help."

COMMUNION SUNDAY

The magic of a meal

Luke 13:22-30

To receive communion is to say with one's body that he or she is ready and willing to share the love that holy meal implies.

One little three-letter word, "eat," is no doubt lost in the bluster of Luke 13:22-30 — a passage laced with weeping and judgment, closed doors and the ominous "the first shall be the last and the last first." Its context is: "People will come from east and west, from north and south and will eat in the kingdom of God." (For "kingdom," read "rule.") What an appealing image given the diplomatic wreckage of the world.

In this passage, Luke is picking up on his predecessor Matthew's condemnation of those Judeans who rejected Jesus as messiah. They're the same ones Luke depicts as being shut out and themselves rejected. Perhaps Luke later found that notion mistaken. Maybe the parable of the prodigal son (Luke 15:11-32) is his correction.

The appealing part of the picture is the procession of outsiders coming from all points of the compass to eat under the rule of God — that rule being characterized by the human behavior mandated in Jesus' ethic of the second mile, the forgiven enemy, the turned cheek and the gladly given coat and cloak. And under such conditions people come to eat. Why is eating so important?

If you discount fast food on the run or rifling the refrigerator between meals, eating is a shared activity. Whom do we invite to our table but those we love, appreciate and care for? We ask family, friends, those who are congenial. Why? Because eating is one of the most intimate of activities. Whom one eats with tells us who is important to whom. The magic wrought by a thoughtfully prepared and tasty meal enjoyed by family and friends at table should not be underestimated.

Luke's point, though, seems to be that under the rule of God, each person is not only friend but family. Under the rule of God (and we're not there yet), our tables would be populated by any and all. We would not hesitate to take in the ragged beggar and eat with him — not merely feed him on the back stoop, if at all. We would sit at table with the homeless of the shelter or the soup kitchen, rather than warily passing out food to them through a window, safely separated from their threatening poverty by a sturdy counter.

That helps makes sense of "the first will be last and the last first." It means that under the rule of God, there will be neither first nor last as in a bread line or soup kitchen queue. There will just be a commodious table around which we'll all sit down, family-style, share what there is and be thankful.

Of course, that is the meaning of the highly symbolic action of the holy communion as together we eat and drink from a common table, a common plate and a common cup. There is, moreover, always enough and to spare.

What a congregation does on a Sunday morning at the Eucharist is a sign of Luke's vision of all humanity gathered as a family under the rule of God. We're not there yet, but the purpose of a Christian congregation is to move ever closer to it.

This sermon is written as the bishops of the Anglican Communion adjourn the 1998 session of the once-a-decade Lambeth Conference at which they dithered over issues of sexuality as if the world around them weren't starved for true and focused moral leadership on issues that really count. It is written as bombs rain down upon Iraq, as embassies pick up the pieces after terrorist bombings. Taken together, these events make for a very unstable world.

If ever there was a hunger and thirst for the realization of the Lucan vision of people coming from east and west and from north and south to eat under the rule of God, it is now. I do not know where the realization of such a vision begins unless it begins here, with us. Let no one come forth today to receive the Eucharistic bread and wine who is not at the same time ready to extend to anyone the love implicit in this meal, who is not prepared to extend the rule of God in his or her life in anticipation of the gathering into unity of the people of the earth.

ADVENT SUNDAY

What can it mean to say "Jesus is coming again"?

Matthew 24:37-44

When and where the hungry are fed, the homeless are sheltered, and the poor and rejected are borne up in charity, Jesus has come again.

In the words of the Nicene Creed, we say of Jesus: "He will come again in glory to judge the living and the dead." We say it; but do we mean it? And do any two of us mean the same thing by it? The return to the human sphere of history by Jesus has long been the overarching theme of Advent — the seasonal run-up to Christmas. The question is whether that theme is a matter of symbolism or literal expectation. I can tell you that, in some quarters of Christianity, it is a matter of literal expectation, literally as various

Bible passages describe it, graphically as Hollywood would film it. Therein, of course, lies difficulty, for if it is literally that Jesus is to come again, he will have to come from somewhere — either where he is now or once again through the process of human conception, gestation and birth.

Where would he be now? The rational answer is that what remains of his remains are somewhere in Palestine, and as far as we know people do not come back from that state of being. In order for Jesus to return through the human birth process, he would have to be fathered by whoever his father had been and delivered of whoever his mother was, meaning that both of them would have to come back from the dead genetically intact — and even then a child they conceived would be yet another person. So what can it mean to say that Jesus will come again?

The biblical image of a celestial Christ descending from cloven skies is, of course, appealing to those who want some otherworldly intervention into human history. And for those who anticipate judgment as an effect of such a coming (usually the judgment of others), it fills a need for closure. Regardless, it must be said by rational people that the so-called "second coming" is at best symbolic as a hope and at worst a potentially dangerous delusion. It encourages the neglect of real-world problems by implying that it doesn't much matter what happens here and now because the second coming will have an essentially magical effect. Also because we know, when in our right minds, that there is no "up there" to come back from.

So what does it mean to say that Jesus is coming again? Can it mean anything that makes sense? Try this on for size: The mission of the church is fundamentally to institute and maintain a rule of life in which all persons are respected, deemed of ultimate worth and cherished. That rule puts love and charity, care and concern for the other at the forefront. That rule sums up one of Jesus' better-known sayings (perhaps a parallel to one of Hillel's): As you would have done to you, do to others. That is the essential thing the Jesus of history seems to have been about. The institution that has been built up around him and his wisdom has more often than not obscured and perverted the image of the person and the purity of his wisdom.

If Christians begin to understand that the church's doctrines, traditions and customs are not ends in themselves but means to an end, and if they understand that that end is to foster the universal, nonsectarian ethic of love of neighbor as of self which Jesus taught and evidently embodied, then it can be said in some rational sense that Jesus is coming again, that at long last what he set forth in the first place is coming into its own as the rule under which human beings willingly live.

No celestial pyrotechnics, no skies rent asunder by the apocalypse, no Dante-esque judgment, no wailing and gnashing of teeth — just lions lying down with lambs, and innocent children playing safely over the adder's nest, people beating swords into plowshares and spears into pruning hooks.

It would be something akin to the Eden the Genesis writer envisioned for the mythical beginning of things, a believable, workable, accessible Eden which could truly be said to be the teaching of Jesus in practice. Only then would it be credible in any sense — and then only symbolically — to say that Jesus is coming again.

In the meantime, the task is to focus on the ministry that is proper to followers of Jesus, to make all we are and do as members of the church become the trip-valve of the cataract, thus causing justice to flow down like waters and righteousness as an ever-flowing stream.

That makes especially of Advent a season of intentional giving of self and resources to the obvious tasks at hand. Or as the Apostle James saw it: "Religion that is pure and undefiled is this: to care for orphans and widows in distress." That at least is a good starting place.

Jesus may not be coming again any time soon, but the holiday celebrating his birth is less than a month away. Is it then clear what we are to do?

CHRISTMAS

Beyond the holly and the ivy

Luke 2:1-20

What would Christmas and its celebration resemble if we took its theme seriously? The event that Christmas supposedly memorializes was not necessarily a pretty one.

Of course, we have no idea of where or when or under what circumstances Jesus was born. We know why Matthew and Luke place the birth in Bethlehem: It was the city from which King David supposedly came, and the Davidic monarchy — impeachable as it might have been, given Bathsheba Lewinsky — was the benchmark against which all subsequent regimes were measured. The messiah, it was said, would come from the house and city of David. So if Jesus (of Nazareth, mind you) was to be portrayed as the anointed one, it would be necessary to assert that he was born in Bethlehem.

As for his lineage, who knows? Was he a descendant of David or of Abraham? It was primarily to Matthew that such a lineage and such a birthplace were important because Matthew's mission was to connect Jesus to as many Hebrew scripture passages as possible to persuade his Antiochan Syrian community of diaspora Jews that Jesus and his way were orthodox. Luke merely took Matthew's particulars and embellished them to serve his purposes. Other New Testament writers mention neither the birth nor the birthplace.

It is Luke's story that we traditionally hear at this season. Its imagery has informed the keeping of Christmas in our time. We add to it Matthew's highly dubious story of Persian astrologers coming across the desert to worship a child-king. And there it all is, complete with beards of cotton and cast-off bathrobes in every church's Sunday school pageant. And it is many people's firm idea of how it actually happened. Luke's creative genius has completely captured the collective imagination. So the question to ask is, what did Luke mean by telling that story? What's its point?

The answer to that question may lie in the elegantly mixed metaphor of these images:

- an infant of royal potential born in a cattle feeding trough in an outbuilding of a cheap hotel in a minor city;
- divine messengers appearing en masse to bring the astounding message of the messiah's advent to shepherds — people at the bottom of the socioeconomic heap. To what does that add up?

It adds up to an upside-down picture that is directly related to Luke's exquisitely political phraseology: "He hath put down the mighty from their seats, and hath exalted the humble and meek." Is Luke in his or her inimitable way telling us that Jesus in his ethical teaching about how the world can best work ("turn the other cheek, walk the second mile, give your one shirt as well as your one coat, forgive as many times as it takes") represents the divine design for peace on Earth among people of goodwill?

Does his tableau of the angels and shepherds say

that God as Luke imagined is concerned first with the poor, that God is not impartial, that God does take sides? So take another look at the nativity scene. Focus on the manger and the livestock. Get the smell into the membranes of your nostrils. Thereby does Luke engage our collective imagination with his word picture.

Now we have to live with the consequences of what it means beyond the sentiment it engenders. And those consequences go way beyond the seasonal charities with which we are familiar. Those treat the symptoms of poverty and destitution. What we need to do for the long term is to change the system so that the mighty, even if they are not to be put down from their seats, must yield the advantage to the humble and meek who, as Jesus said, are after all the blessed.

So Luke's story, despite its fictional elements, enshrines a deep and abiding truth that emerged from the desert faith of Israel and came to fruition in the prophets and, finally, in Jesus of Nazareth. And that truth is that religion as it is known at least by Jews and Christians has everything to do with economics, public policy and politics where the care and welfare of disadvantaged people are concerned. That's what Luke and his nativity story are telling us. It is at the core of this feast's significance — around, behind and beyond the holly and the ivy.

EPIPHANY

A multitude of camels shall cover you

Matthew 2:1-12

Maybe the story of the Wise Men is political theater. It would be as if the U.S. secretary of state were to go to some minor, vexatious Third World nation and kneel humbly before its rulers. Think about it.

The unlikely title of this homily is one of my favorite images in the Bible. It is part of the Third Isaiah's triumphant vision of a post-exilic Israel in a time when all wounds are healed, when its people have recovered from the grievances borne over generations of siege and subjugation. A multitude of camels would cover its territory, camels from all over bearing goods along the north-south trade routes of Palestine — making it no longer a wide spot in the road but a thriving junction. The prophets always did understand Israel's deliverance in economic terms.

Yet the Third Isaiah's optimistic vision was never realized in biblical times, and the jury is still out as to whether contemporary Israel-Palestine will realize it.

The New Testament writer Matthew picked up on the prophetic theme of Israel's hoped-for economic and political vindication in the familiar story of Persian court magicians coming to Judea to worship a child they believed to be a future king. At the time Matthew confected that story, it would have been as sensational as it now seems improbable. He wrote within a decade or so of the epoch-making destruction of the Jerusalem Temple by the world's then ruling power. Israel-Judea had once again — and apocalyptically — been brought to its knees.

The image of important personages from an ancient and grand kingdom coming to do homage to a Hebrew child would have — and no doubt did — become a rallying cry for some of a confused and defeated people. (We need to remember that, in all probability, Matthew's audience and community was largely comprised of Diaspora Jews.)

Put contemporary Christianity of the kind that values and maybe even models economic justice into that context, and you have a version of events that is somewhat parallel to those that were unfolding in the latter part of the first century: a political juggernaut arrayed against a largely economically disenfranchised citizenry.

The depredations of Roman occupation in that era are well-known. A number of contemporary New Testament scholars — notably John Dominic Crossan — have presented a convincing hypothesis that those events are what brought John the Baptizer and Jesus into public life as resisters of that oppression. We see how immediately successful they were: John ended up having his head separated from his body; Jesus was gibbeted. Matthew's story of the Magi thus becomes underground resistance...

... which is how the story might be read by late 20th-century Christians who, if they are not, ought to be organized against the heartless capitalism that so often puts primary value on profit and stock values over the interests and welfare of middle- and lower-class workers, not to mention the unemployed.

Such resistance will inevitably be only marginally successful at best, and a spectacular failure at worst — which doesn't mean we should give up. We're certainly not going to look or be more successful than Israel-Judea was in the Third Isaiah's time or Diaspora Jews in Matthew's time.

A multitude of camels did not cover them and will not cover us — even with the much-touted North American Free Trade Agreement. No exotic strangers will come among us seeking messiah. No celestial messenger will come to rest over where we work day by day, week by week and year by year. Our cause — economic justice — is not popular because it's too costly, doesn't reward the already powerful and doesn't make headlines.

What keeps the cause alive is the belief that, however hopeless it sometimes seems, it is right. And if the bible is right, we might go so far as to say it is of God. Because if religion is about anything that matters, it is about what we do for others as a community centered on the ethical wisdom of Jesus — he who was derided, criticized, persecuted and, finally, executed for the cause we've been talking about.

That's why it is important to hear and hear again Isaiah's "multitude of camels" imagery and Matthew's outrageous story about Persian courtesans traveling to Nowheresville to worship a child of peasant birth. Neither thing happened, but each might have. It is possible that the valleys will be lifted up and the mountains and hills will be made low. Just because it looks well-nigh impossible doesn't mean it is.

LENT

Adam & Eve, Señor Snake and original sin

Matthew 5:13-20

Human beings, as part of the natural order, are works in progress with both potential good and potential evil within them. The key is to nurture the former and eradicate the latter in the quest for order.

This just might be the time to say it: The Doctrine of Original Sin is one of the most useless and intellectually corrupt inventions of the human mind. The idea that what some early humanoid did or failed to do has indelibly marked me or my children is nonsense.

It should not escape our attention that the two quite different and contradictory myths of creation found in the book of Genesis disagree about human beginnings. The older version, which includes the Adam and Eve and Cain and Abel narratives, essentially sees human beginnings as flawed — sinful, in fact. The later version depicts the gods as pronouncing the entirety of their creation "very good."

What biblical theologians have wrongly done is to say that, indeed, the gods (or God) created everything as good but that later man (you should excuse the expression) despoiled it in rebellious behavior — thus blending two contradictory, unblendable stories. Reason and common sense suggest that if a purposeful creator having the kind of power generally attributed to God undertook to create human beings, no major mistakes would have been made.

The implication of the Adam-and-Eve-in-the-garden story is that something big went haywire early on that caused the human being to be other that what its creator intended. Adam and Eve's thirst for knowledge, aided and abetted by a wily serpent, was construed as a crime proceeding from an unavoidable tragic flaw in the human makeup. The punishment has become the punishment of all descendants.

This presents two problems:

1) A just God would not set in motion an evolutionary process that produced human consciousness and intelligence but forbade its seeking knowledge. Or, if you want to go with the other meaning of the verb "to know," a just God would not set in motion a process that produced the instinctual desire for physical gratification but forbade its contemplation and realization.

2) A just God would not punish me for what you did or you for what I did, much less my children. Punishment is an emotionally loaded word that means "consequences," as in Newton's proven dictum that every action has an equal and opposite reaction. True, sometimes residual consequences ensue. If I run a red light as you are passing the intersection on green, I may go to jail. You may go to the hospital or perhaps beyond. But it is not punishment decreed by a heavenly tribunal. In either case, it is consequences.

Now here's a question: Why does the Genesis writer who gave us Adam and Eve locate evil and the cause of the primal couple's tragic flaw in a talking, walking snake? Remember, the serpent was condemned to slither about upon his belly only after his complicity in the Forbidden Fruit caper.

Human begins are wont to look for exterior sources of evil rather than understand that they, like all in the natural order, are evolving beings, works in progress. Perfection eludes the uncompleted, for the word "perfect" means "finished." And what is finished in this fluid world? Even the granite faces of ancient mountains are undergoing change, however invisible to the eye, however glacially.

As we begin Lent, which is the appointed time to meditate upon our unfinished, incomplete and imperfect nature, what can we intelligently make of the ideas of sin, temptation and evil?

First, we remember that they are symbols for sometimes intangible realities that defy naming and accounting for. Second, we remember that their imagery derives from other times not our own. Third, we apply our late 20th-century powers of reason and knowledge to their interpretation and seek to deal with the realities behind them in appropriate ways: through psychological or psychiatric counseling or treatment; through education, negotiation, moral example, even through intelligent and selective force as we may have to deal with the likes of Saddam Hussein and the butchers of Serbia.

If you're looking for the serpent, look for it coiled within as a part of our unfinished nature, as part of that chaos over which we believe the God of the Bible continues to brood and from which that God brings order. We may become God's partners by seeking and working for moral order in everything we are and do. In fact, I think it is correct to say that if being found in the image of God means anything, it means that our purpose is to achieve order internally in ourselves and externally in the world.

So you can give up chocolate or popcorn for the next six weeks and call it Lent if you want. However, it would be more to the point to discover where you can make a difference and become with God an orderer of chaos.

PALM SUNDAY

When the going gets tough

Matthew 26:36-27:66

Jesus' path is not a graded superhighway but a tortuous way. It's more uphill than down with plenty of obstacles and potential danger. It is not for the faint of heart.

I don't suppose it was ever particularly easy for Jesus once he had set his course in life. Once he decided that social and economic justice were absolutely central to what he took to be the divine mandate, there was no turning back.

He saw that the occupation armies of Rome and their military governments had not the least concern for his people's welfare and that, therefore, his people would have to respond to the inevitable by intentionally caring for each other. You'd think that would be a fairly simple and straightforward point. But in trying to make that point, Jesus hit the wall, and it finally toppled upon him.

Economics is a minefield, especially when you're telling people that what they do with their resources is not a private but a community matter. Jesus' admonition to give up your one shirt as well as your one coat was spoken to those who stood on the poverty side of the line. Those completely destitute stood on the other side.

That kind of economics — a kind of socialism — alarmed and offended people, even people to whom Jesus was not speaking directly. Coupled with his ethic of passive resistance (as in "turn the other cheek"), with his ethic of accommodation (as in "walk the second mile"), with his ethic of no-strings-attached charity (as in "love your enemies"), Jesus' economics made him at once a charismatic and a threatening figure.

In the same way, Mohandas Gandhi and Martin Luther King Jr. were both charismatic and threatening. And when that is realized by enough people, the going gets tough. The ones whose names we remember — as in Jesus, Gandhi and King — are the ones who never wavered from the path, who stayed their course even unto death.

That's the theme of Holy Week — the walk from the city gate of Jerusalem to the Via Dolorossa and out the gate opposite and on up the hill called Calvary. At any number of junctures even before that fateful entry into the holy city, Jesus could have caved. When and where the going got tough, he could have chucked it and saved himself a lot of grief. So could Gandhi have. So could King have. They are remembered, celebrated and revered because they did not.

"Let those who would come after me," Jesus said, "take up their own cross and follow me." Is that something that was attributed to Jesus by the gospel writers long after the crucifixion, or did Jesus, aware of that peculiarly dreadful means of execution, figure that it was where he was headed anyway, as were any who stayed the course with him?

We remember Jesus and suffer ourselves to march under his banner because even the specter of crucifixion did not daunt him. But we cannot for very long so march unless we ourselves are ready to pay the price of ostracism and loss. As in Jesus' time, so in ours, injustices cry out for redress. Homeless people sleep in the street. Children suffer in poverty. Millions live in fear of sickness because they have no health insurance. You could go on and on.

To take on such causes against the tidal wave of heartless capitalism and its evil political twin is to court the very consequences that befell Jesus ... and Gandhi ... and King.

So take a walk on the Via Dolorossa and spend a while at the Wailing Wall. Look over the shoulder and see the Cross waiting on Calvary. The going has just gotten tough. Do we follow him or not?

EASTER

The women told them

Luke 24:1-10

You may think Easter is about resuscitated bodies, at least One in particular. It may be more about setting you free. See what you think.

If Easter is about anything, it is about being new, fresh and unprecedented. It is about freedom and liberty and the joy in which both partake. For us in the northern hemisphere, at least, Easter means — or at least promises — spring, which, in turn, promises the fullness of summer.

For Christians, Easter is a day of hope that transcends the ordinary and predictable. That is the sense of the language of this day and season. The third evangelist, Luke, is a major contributor to that literature, and it is from his work that we hear on this Easter the resurrection story.

In no important way does Luke's version differ from others that we know. We have an empty grave and the strong suggestion that it is empty because its former occupant has no further use for it. Two men — Luke means for us to understand that they are divine messengers — garbed in dazzling vestments have this to say: "He is not here, but has risen."

The discerning reader will soon discover how skilled a storyteller Luke is. He framed this story, and bookended it with narratives about women. The women are the ones earlier identified as those who had come with Jesus from Galilee to Jerusalem. Luke's Easter story begins with them and ends with them.

They approach Jesus' grave to make the final preparation of the corpse for permanent interment. It was to the women that the heavenly messengers revealed the truth: "He is not here, but has risen." Luke is telling us that just as his shepherds in Chapter 2 heard the news of Jesus' birth from angelic heralds, so now women are hearing the news of his triumph over human cruelty, injustice and over death itself.

Need we take any time at all to recall what lowly stations in life shepherds and women — for different reasons — occupied in first-century Palestine? In Luke's plot, the shepherds apparently kept their news to themselves, being content with a brief visit to the manger. The women in the cemetery, however, are made out to be the first century's version of CNN on the spot. Luke deliberately writes: "Now it was Mary Magdalene, Joanna, Mary the mother of James and other women with them who told this to the apostles."

Oh, how Luke toys with us and with his late first-century audience. "Apostles" are the ones who tell the good news, not a gaggle of excitable women. Moreover, all the official apostles turn out to be men.

The word "apostle" is associated with second-generation leadership of the infant church. It means "one sent out," sent out with a message of which he or she is not the originator but a carrier. The key to the whole passage is the astonishing (for the first century) claim that women told the future apostles the most important piece of news ever.

What a new, unprecedented, liberating story this becomes in that light. Luke is saying that Jesus, both in life and death, brought liberation — in this case the liberation of the heretofore oppressed 50 percent of the human race, liberation of a kind no amount of legislation could ever grant.

So it is that on Easter in a half-dozen dioceses of the Episcopal Church in the United States, women who are bishops are preaching the gospel and presiding at the liturgy — women who are the true successors of the first apostles who, Luke implies, were women. Truly the Easter gospel is a gospel of liberation.

Whatever fear or fetter has you in its grip, today's gospel is a reminder that you can be liberated from it if you want:

- a fear of death or what happens afterward.
- a fear of life and what might happen next.
- a fear of what may happen if you take that next step.
- a fear of trusting, a fear of braving ambiguity and uncertainty with courage.

The raising of Jesus from the dead as the gospels imply but never describe is a metaphor for liberation and victory. It makes the impossible possible, the undoable doable, the unbelievable believable.

A bibliographic note

It is fair to ask where a preacher is coming from. Are his/her sermons just passing surmise and airy opinion? I can speak only for myself. The answer to both questions is "no." My sermons invariably emerge from the careful reading of a particular text but always in the larger context of a passage or an entire document. For example, one cannot adequately understand a text, say, from Luke without an appreciation of Luke's theological agenda and the sources which lay behind the writer's work.

For most of the last 40 years I have lived with biblical texts — particularly those of the gospels — in the languages in which we first received them (Hebrew, Aramaic and Greek). I have translated as best I could each text I have ever used homiletically. Translations accomplished in the mid-1960s vary some from ones recently made as scholarship in the field has evolved.

Invaluable aids to textual analysis are the biblical commentaries that perform the exegetical work right on the page. The most accessible of these are the Interpreter's Bible series, which is even now being rewritten and issued volume by volume. Volumes VIII and IX of the New Interpreter's Bible covering the four canonical gospels are now in print. Their exegesis and exposition are fresh and reflect the marvelous biblical scholarship of the last 35 to 40 years.

Beyond the commentaries are other substantive works which are bound to affect a homiletician's work. I mention just a few here which are relatively recent and available in most mainline bookstores. In no particular order of importance, they include:

- **Matthew** (Vol. 26 of the Anchor Bible Series) by W.F. Albright and C.S. Mann
- **An Introduction to the New Testament** by Raymond E. Brown

- **The Birth of the Messiah** by Raymond E. Brown
- **The Death of the Messiah** by Raymond E. Brown
- **The Gospel of John** (Vols. 29 and 29a, Anchor Bible Series) by Raymond E. Brown
- **Theology of the Old Testament** by Walter Brueggemann
- **The Gospel of John** by Rudolf Bultmann
- **The Other Gospels,** ed. Ron Cameron
- **The Historical Jesus** by John Dominic Crossan
- **Who Killed Jesus?** by John Dominic Crossan
- **Who Is Jesus?** by John Dominic Crossan
- **The Birth of Christianity** by John Dominic Crossan
- **The Gospel According to Luke** (Vols. 28 and 28a of the Anchor Bible Series) by Joseph A. Fitzmyer
- **Honest to Jesus** by Robert Funk
- **The Five Gospels,** ed. Robert Funk, Roy Hoover, et. al

- **The Formation of Q** by John Kloppenborg
- **The Lost Gospel** by Burton L. Mack
- **Mark** (Vol. 27 of the Anchor Bible Series) by C.S. Mann
- **The First Urban Christians** by Wayne Meeks
- **A Marginal Jew** by John P. Meier
- **Binding the Strong Man** by Chad Myers
- **The Gnostic Gospels** by Elaine Pagels
- **The Origin of Satan** by Elaine Pagels
- **Adam, Eve and the Serpent** by Elaine Pagels
- **Jesus and the Victory of God** by N.T. Wright

ABOUT THE AUTHOR

Harry T. Cook is rector of St. Andrew's Episcopal Church in Clawson, Michigan, and a former journalist, editor and columnist. He is known for his teaching ministry in biblical studies and for his provocative and often controversial sermons.

He is a graduate of Albion (Mich.) College and Garrett-Evangelical Theological Seminary at Northwestern University in Evanston, Ill.

Cook is also the author of *Christianity Beyond Creeds,* an analysis of traditional beliefs and their restatement in terms compatible with our own time.